RUBANK EDUCATIONAL L[

RUBANK
Advanced Method

DRUMS

HARVEY S. WHISTLER

AN ADVANCED COURSE OF STUDY

DESIGNED TO FOLLOW UP ANY

OF THE VARIOUS ELEMENTARY

AND INTERMEDIATE METHODS

RUBANK®

HAL•LEONARD®
CORPORATION
7777 W. BLUEMOUND RD. P.O. BOX 13819 MILWAUKEE, WI 53213

PREFACE

Designed to follow any of the Elementary or Intermediate methods currently used, the **Rubank Advanced Method for Drums** is a complete course of study, embracing not only a review of the well-known Twenty-Six Rudiments of drumming, but also presenting many valuable exercises, etudes, and musical excerpts, all of which have been written expressly for the purpose of developing on the part of the students studying them, a high degree of technical skill and musical proficiency in the art of percussion playing.

Too much stress cannot be placed upon the mastery of the twenty-six rudiments, referred to above. It is true that an advanced course of study is not the place in which to explain and teach these rudiments, for they should be covered fully in an elementary or intermediate drum method; however, before proceeding with the present course, a review of these rudiments should be undertaken.

An adjunct to any advanced course of drum study is a course in tympani playing, and students completing the present work, who are not acquainted with the tympani, should take up the study of this all-important set of instruments at once. For such purposes, an introduction to tympani playing is provided in the **Rubank Elementary Tympani Method.**

If the **Rubank Advanced Method for Drums** proves itself a boon to those in quest of material to aid in solving the many problems that confront the present day instructors of percussion instruments, whether they be private teachers of such instruments, or public school music directors, the writer will feel gratified to know that his earnest efforts have been of at least some educational significance.

HARVEY S. WHISTLER

Twenty-Six Essential Rudiments of Drumming

> Ability to execute the first thirteen of these rudiments is a requirement for membership in the National Association of Rudimental Drummers.

HARVEY S. WHISTLER

Rudiment No.1: Long Roll

Rudiment No.2: Five-Stroke Roll

Rudiment No.3: Seven-Stroke Roll

Rudiment No.4: Flam

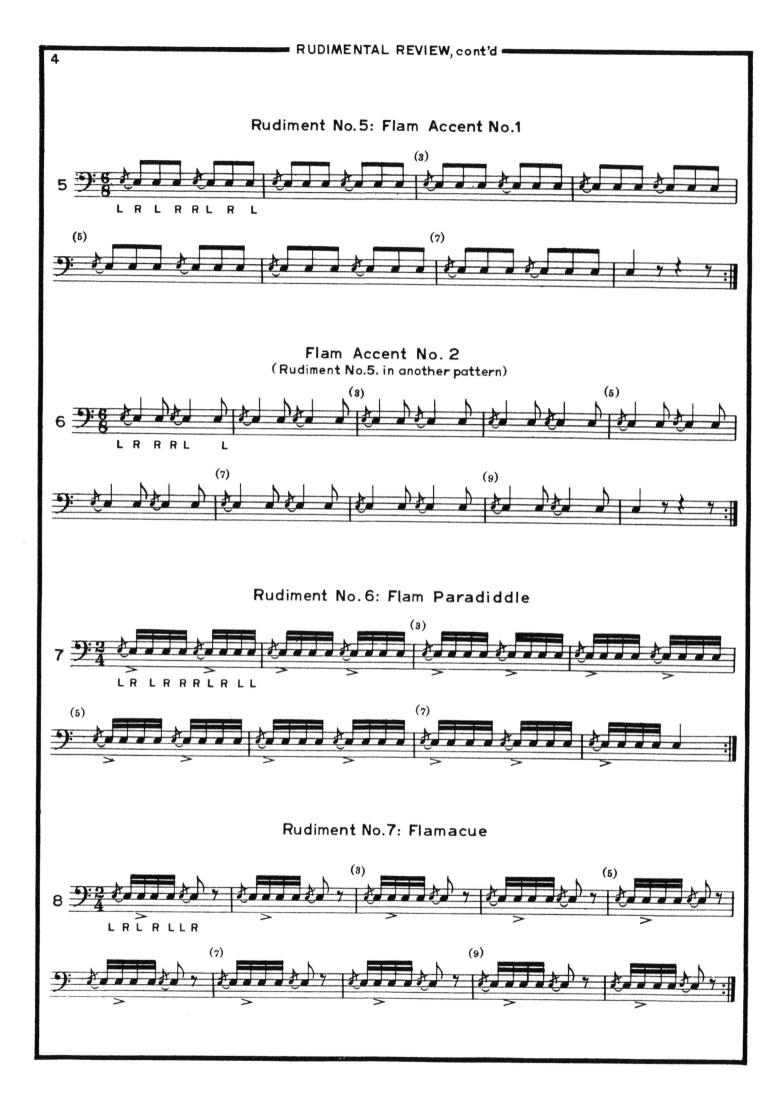

Rudiment No.8: Ruff

Rudiment No.9: Single Drag

Rudiment No.10: Double Drag

Rudiment No.11: Double Paradiddle

Rudiment No.12: Single Ratamacue

Rudiment No.13: Triple Ratamacue

Rudiment No.14: Single-Stroke Roll

Rudiment No.15: Nine-Stroke Roll

Rudiment No.16: Ten-Stroke Roll

Rudiment No.17: Eleven-Stroke Roll

Rudiment No.18: Thirteen-Stroke Roll

Rudiment No.19: Fifteen-Stroke Roll

Rudiment No. 20: Flam Tap

Rudiment No. 21: Single Paradiddle

Rudiment No. 22: Drag Paradiddle No. 1

Rudiment No. 23: Drag Paradiddle No. 2

Rudiment No. 24: Flam Paradiddle-Diddle

Rudiment No. 25: Ratatap

Commonly known as "Lesson No 25," this rudiment recently was designated the "Ratatap," this name being given to it by the eminent drum authority, William F. Ludwig

Ratatap
Rudiment No 25 in another pattern

Rudiment No. 26: Double Ratamacue

10

Rhythmical Studies in $\frac{2}{4}$ Time (Meter)

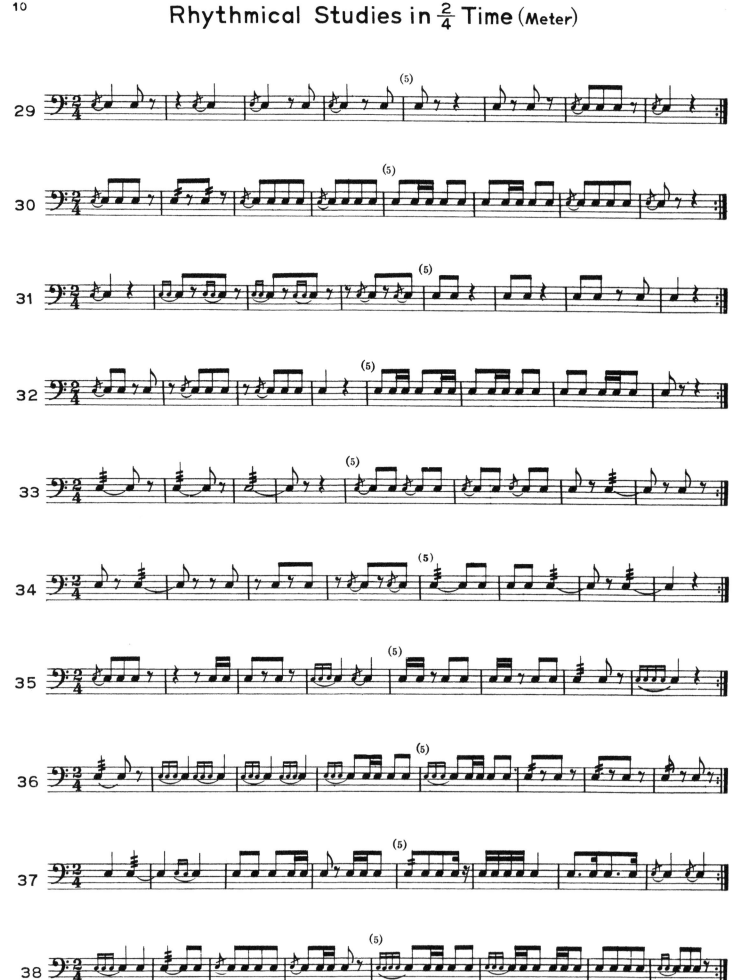

11

Rhythmical Studies in ¾ Time (Meter)

Rhythmical Studies in 4/4 or Common Time (Meter)

Six Solo Etudes for Snare Drum

ETUDE TRIUMPHANT

Rhythmical Studies in $\frac{3}{8}$ Time (Meter)

Rhythmical Studies in $\frac{6}{8}$ Time (Meter)

Rhythmical Studies in $\frac{9}{8}$ Time (Meter)

Rhythmical Studies in $\frac{12}{8}$ Time (Meter)

Six Solo Etudes for Snare Drum

ETUDE TRIUMPHANT

ETUDE HEROIC

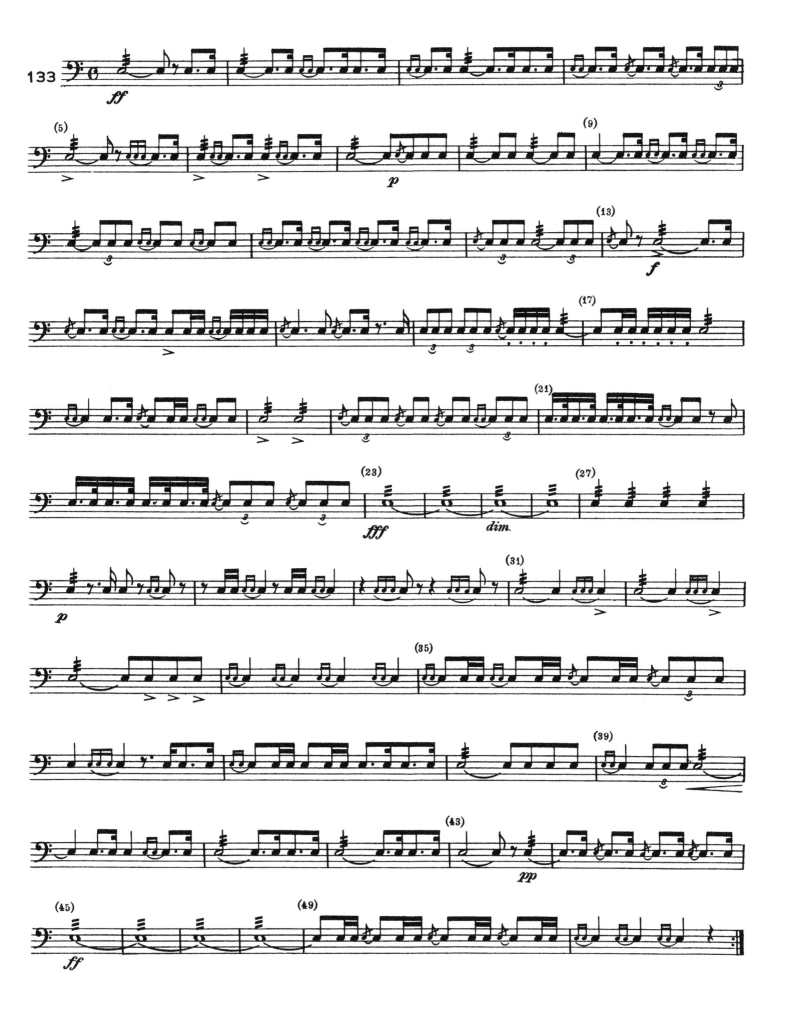

ETUDE MAJESTIC

ETUDE SYMPHONIQUE

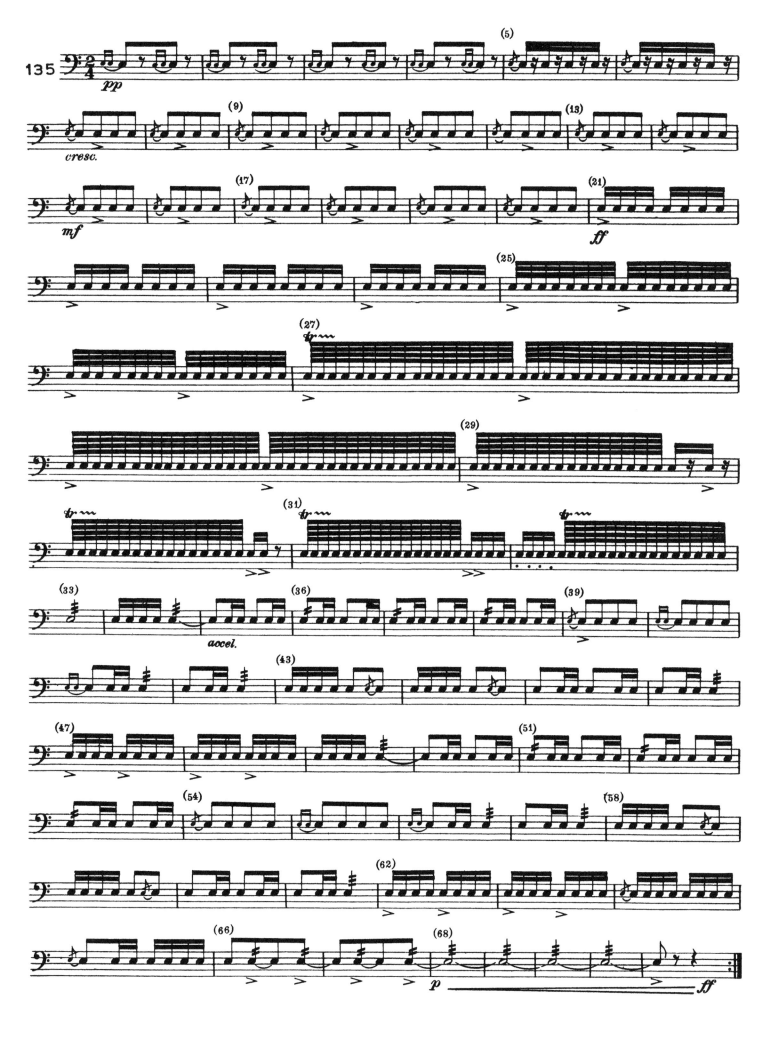

ETUDE de BALLET No.1

ETUDE de BALLET No.2

Orchestral Solos for Snare Drum

SOLO from FAUST

GOUNOD

SOLO from RIENZI

WAGNER

Repeat from beginning

SOLO from L'AFRICAINE

MEYERBEER

140

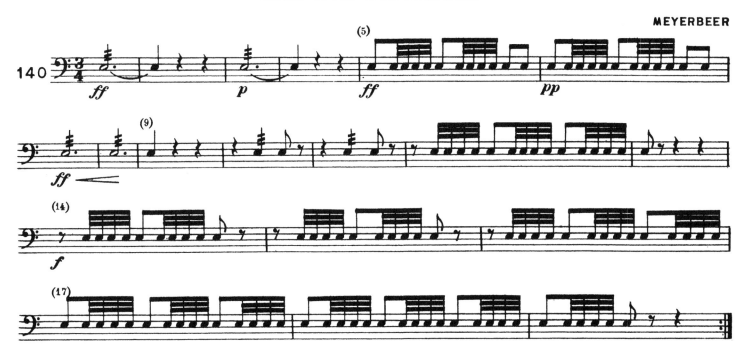

SOLO from THE PROPHET

MEYERBEER

Tempo di marcia maestoso

141

28

SOLO from CARMEN

Allegro moderato

BIZET

SOLO from ATHALIA

MENDELSSOHN

Allegro vivace

SOLO from PIQUE DAME

von SUPPE

SOLO from MASANIELLO

AUBER

Allegro moderato

SOLO from THE BOHEMIAN GIRL

BALFE

Orchestral Solos for Bass Drum

SOLO from DAUGHTER OF THE REGIMENT

DONIZETTI

SOLO from RIGOLETTO

VERDI

SOLO from TRAVIATA

VERDI

Orchestral Solos for Bass Drum and Cymbals

SOLO from SYMPHONY PATHETIQUE

TSCHAIKOWSKY

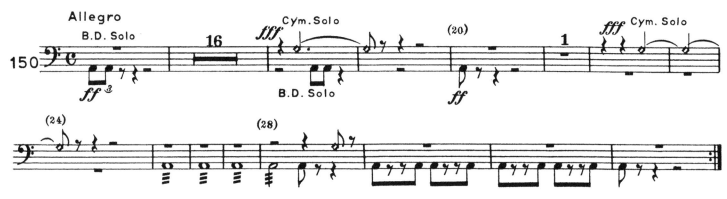

SOLO from HUNGARIAN RHAPSODY No.2

LISZT

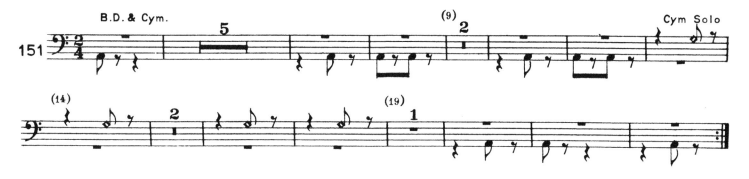

SOLO from DIE MEISTERSINGER

Allegro

WAGNER

Repeat from beginning

Orchestral Solos for Triangle

EXTRACTS from CARMEN

BIZET

EXTRACTS from THE PROPHET

MEYERBEER

Orchestral Solo for Triangle, Bass Drum and Cymbals

LIBUSE OVERTURE

SMETANA

Orchestral Solo for Triangle, Snare Drum, Bass Drum and Cymbals

THE MOLDAU

SMETANA

Orchestral Solo for Tambourine

EXTRACTS from CARMEN

BIZET

Orchestral Solo for Triangle, Cymbals, Castanets, Tambourine and Drums

BACCHANALE from SAMSON and DELILAH

SAINT-SAENS

Band and Orchestral Selections for Drums

THE TEMPEST from RIGOLETTO

DRUMS

VERDI

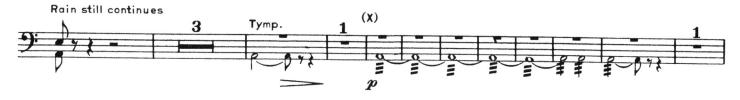

El Choclo
Tango Argentino

A.G.VILLOLDO
Arr. by Ed Chenette

Drums-Castanets

Father of Victory
March

L. GANNE
Arr. by Ed Chenette

Drums

Tally Ho!
Selection

HERMAN A. HUMMEL

Drums

Prince Methusalem Overture

Drums

JOHANN STRAUSS

Allegro moderato

Poco piu

Maestoso

(M)

Allegretto

(N)

Allegro

Piu allegro

Jolly Robbers Overture

Drums

von SUPPE

El Matador

Spanish March

Drums

CASTRO CARAZO

165

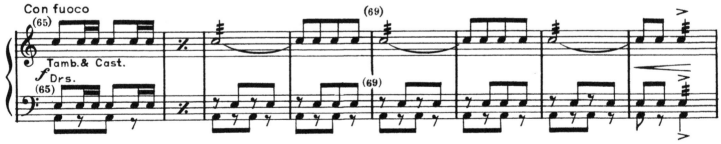